AMAZING STORIES

EMILY CARR

AMAZING STORIES

EMILY CARR

The Incredible Life and Adventures
of a West Coast Artist

HISTORY/BIOGRAPHY
by Cat Klerks

PUBLISHED BY ALTITUDE PUBLISHING CANADA LTD.
1500 Railway Avenue, Canmore, Alberta T1W 1P6
www.altitudepublishing.com
1-800-957-6888

Publisher	Stephen Hutchings
Associate Publisher	Kara Turner
Editor	Audrey McClellan

We acknowledge the financial support of the Government
of Canada through the Book Publishing Industry Development
Program (BPIDP) for our publishing activities.

Altitude GreenTree Program
Altitude Publishing will plant twice as many trees as were used
in the manufacturing of this product.

National Library of Canada Cataloguing in Publication Data
Klerks, Cat
Emily Carr / Cat Klerks ; edited by Audrey A. McClellan.

(Amazing stories)
Includes bibliographical references.
ISBN 1-55153-996-9

1. Carr, Emily, 1871-1945. 2. Painters--Canada--Biography. I. McClellan,
Audrey. II. Title. III. Series: Amazing stories (Canmore, Alta.)
ND249.C3K53 2003   759.11   C2003-910417-6

An application for the trademark for Amazing Stories™
has been made and the registered trademark is pending.

Printed and bound in Canada by Friesens
4 6 8 9 7 5 3

The front cover shows Emily Carr as a young woman
Reproduced courtesy of BC Archives (B-00877)

To my family

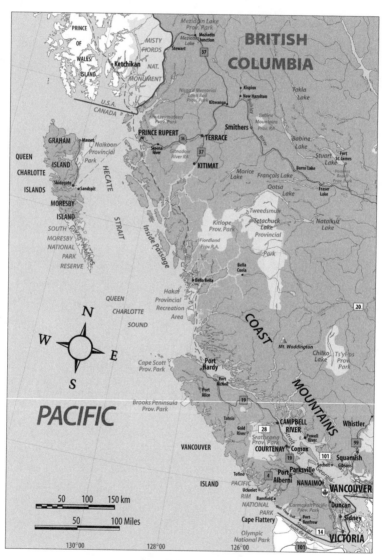

Canada's West Coast

Contents

Prologue *11*

Chapter 1 A European Education 13

Chapter 2 Home Again 35

Chapter 3 The Laughing One 55

Chapter 4 Rebirth 72

Chapter 5 Final Days 90

Epilogue: Emily Carr, Mythmaker . . . 110

Bibliography *113*

Prologue

The rain beat down hard on the tin roof of the caravan, nearly drowning out the hesitant tap-tapping of the typewriter keys. There was a faint smell in the air, not entirely unpleasant, of paint thinner mingled with the warm, rich scent of the forest in summer. An owl hooted. In the corner a puppy stirred, blinked, and fell back to sleep. A white rat in an old shoebox shredded paper ceaselessly, readying a nest for babies that never came.

The woman paused in her work and sighed. In the dim light her slanted grey eyes seemed to gleam, cat-like, as she surveyed her refuge. It was a good night to be indoors. A cougar had been spotted in the woods this morning; there'd be no bathing in the river by moonlight tonight. She allowed a slightly malicious smile to play around her lips. A cougar. That'd keep the fool day-trippers and picnickers out of her hair, for a while at least.

Her face grew suddenly tender as she cast a loving look at Woo, her constant companion for over 15 years. The tiny, wizened monkey in its scarlet dress sat framed by the window, slowly working a needle through a scrap of cloth, absorbed in its work, oblivious, mute. The scene, at once cozy and bizarre, reminded her that soon she would be back to the terrible drudgery of her home life. Soon, this blissful solitude and independence would be gone.

Her fingers flexed over the keyboard. Where to begin? She had visited Dickens' London, Gauguin's France — explored the myth world of the Haida people. There was still so much work to be done, and time was running short. She relaxed, let her mind drift back over the years, and began to write...

Chapter 1
A European Education

I t was a homecoming, of sorts.

Since childhood, Emily Carr had been brought up to worship all things English. The clothes, the manners, the culture — all, she had been taught by her British-born parents, were the finest things a young lady from Victoria, British Columbia, could ever aspire to. Though she had spent three years studying art in San Francisco and five more eking out a living as an art instructor in BC, it was in London that she would begin her training in earnest. A friend had travelled to England to study and had had nothing but good things to say in her letters home.

Canada was wild, unpaintable; England was the apex of culture and learning. Yet Emily loathed it from the moment she staggered, seasick, down the gangplank onto British soil.

On paper, studying in London sounded ideal. It was 1899, the dawn of a new era. What could be more stimulating than being exposed to new concepts in a new setting at a time when the great modern artists were emerging all over Europe? Emily was convinced that people back in Victoria were more interested in being respectable than in exploring new ideas. It was a semi-rural town, with dirt roads and cow pastures, when she entered the world one stormy night in 1871, and it had not changed much by the time she sailed away nearly three decades later. Conformity and love of tradition were the townspeople's most marked traits. To them, painting was a hobby, not a way of life. Emily had been chastised in the past for "playing" at art; now she was determined to show how serious a game it was.

The Westminster School of Art
Emily soon found out that the Westminster School of Art was not the place to learn new ideas either. For someone who loved to paint nature and the outdoors, the school was stuffy and restrictive. She found it even more conservative than the arts scene back home, where old

ladies drank endless cups of tea and congratulated each other on their excellent taste in watercolours. Housed in the tony Architectural Museum, her new school was another monument to stodgy ideas.

On her first day, Emily made an unpleasant discovery. As a new student she would be required to take an Antique class, which entailed drawing replicas of ancient Greek and Roman statues. Her heart sank at the thought. When she was young she had not spent her pocket money on penny candy and hair ribbons like other girls did. Instead, she had gone down to the local tombstone-maker and bought giant plaster casts of human body parts in order to teach herself basic anatomy. She was no longer interested in learning to draw from lifeless statuary, and she was not keen on becoming a "ditch-digger," as she called her fellow students, worshipping the past.

However, the only alternative was to take a Life class, which meant sketching nude models. In an era when a glimpse of a woman's ankle was considered scandalous, this was not a step to be taken lightly. Emily thought of what her family would say if they found out. "They'd have me prayed for in church!" she exclaimed to a friend.

The Life class won out. Emily chose warm, live flesh over cold, hard stone. She was not here to look back, but to move forward. Art history in general bored her. Never a good student, she could not be bothered memorizing names and dates. She was half-amused, half-intimidated by the decrepit stone sculptures — "The Great Ones," she mockingly called them — she passed every day to get to class.

Though modernism was sweeping away the cobwebs of tradition elsewhere in Europe, the London art scene was still steeped in the pretty, pastoral, academic tradition that had gripped it for so long. There were pockets of bohemia scattered throughout the city, where radical young people discussed and promoted new art styles, but Emily never managed to connect with any of them.

Emily's own circle of friends was conservative and respectable. She befriended some of her classmates, but found most of them unapproachable. Fortunately, she had come to London with a handful of letters of introduction to distant relatives and friends of friends. This was how she met Mrs. Redden, who became her closest confidante in England.

Marion Redden was an elderly widow, born in Canada, who now lived in London with her bachelor son. The older woman was both fond and disapproving of her new friend and hoped London would "polish Canada off" her. She took Emily to the National Gallery, hoping to smooth out some of those rough edges herself, but Emily was not impressed. She found it dull and gloomy. It was almost as bad as the British Museum, which she dismissed as "the world mummified." The London Zoo was much more her style.

London, where she had hoped to be able to spread her wings, was turning out to be just as stifling as home. It was noisy, crowded, and dirty, not the haven she had envisioned. Even the San Francisco School of Design, a rat-infested tenement she had quit high school to attend, seemed like paradise in comparison. There she had been exposed to different cultures, had a chance to see a little of the world. Here it seemed there was always someone telling her what to do: teachers who wanted her to paint their way; society ladies who were scandalized by her backward, "colonial" manners; even one young man who sailed all the way from Canada to beg her to give up art and marry him. She was told to go to church, do good works, and associate with all the right people. Every thought, every action, was governed by some kind of code she could not crack. She was nearing 30, but she was still being treated like an impetuous child.

Emily was beginning to wish she had chosen to study in bohemian Paris, not conservative London. It was clear this was not the right environment for her. She could not give up, though. To return to Canada too soon would vindicate all the doubters back home. Emily wanted desperately to prove herself.

She decided to look beyond the confines of the art school and try her hand at commercial art. She took a batch of some of her more charming Canadian-themed sketches to Frederick Warne, publisher of the Beatrix Potter books, hoping to have them printed, perhaps as a calendar. She had one of the letters of introduction clutched in her hand along with her portfolio as she mounted the three flights of stairs to the publisher's headquarters. The treatment she received there would rankle for decades afterward. Instead of being ushered into the office as she had hoped, she had to verbally tussle with a little cockney boy who was determined to keep her as far from his employer as possible. Emily persisted. The "elegant creature" who eventually condescended to meet with her was not enthusiastic about her sketches. Emily was suddenly conscious of her own dowdy appearance and gauche manners. He examined her drawings for a while, then told her she was free to take them right back to Canada, where they belonged. Her career as an illustrator was over before it began.

Slow Decline

A series of frightening experiences further unsettled

Emily while in London. An old foot injury, the result of a childhood accident, flared up, making walking painful. She was forced to take a shortcut to school through an unsavoury part of town, a filthy slum that bordered the Architectural Museum. Her new friends begged her to be careful, knowing the danger she was courting. One foggy morning a street sweeper, a drunken character straight out of a Charles Dickens novel, slammed his broom into her legs, claiming she was "obstructin' a gent's hoccipation." The blow jarred her sore foot and her dress was covered in muck. She was both angry and ashamed. She cursed London and its inhabitants as she hobbled her way to school. Eventually, she had to have a toe amputated, though it did little to relieve the pain.

When Queen Victoria died, Emily took a stool along to the historic funeral procession, thinking she could sit on the sidelines to view it. The streets were so crowded that she was forced to stand, only to be so badly crushed that she fainted dead away. She was bruised and shaken afterward.

Her misfortunes began to wear her down. Emily became irritable and prone to tears, though she did her best to conceal her misery. Eager to escape the hectic pace of the city, she travelled to less cosmopolitan places by the sea and in the country, keeping London as her central base. In the provincial towns, there were always teachers keen to take on a bright, enthusiastic student and new friends to be charmed by a quick wit and pleasant manner. She was happiest when she was around people she could mother, and she was quick to comfort the younger, homesick students. She loved to cheer them up and tease them with funny little poems and drawings.

But her joking manner covered an escalating anxiety. Her health suffered. It began with a tumble down a flight of stairs. Though she was not badly hurt, she took to her bed and could not summon the energy to get up, even after she had recovered from her fall. Years later she said it was like someone had flicked the light switch of her emotions into the "off" position. Though she blamed her state on overwork and her distaste for city life, it was obvious there was something much more serious wrong with her. She developed strange physical symptoms, from blinding headaches and a stutter to numbness in her legs, which caused her to limp. She was constantly nauseated and as weak as a kitten.

Lizzie, her irritatingly religious sister whose dearest wish was to be a missionary and convert the heathens of the world, rushed over from Canada to take care of her ailing sibling. But Lizzie aggravated and quarrelled with Emily, deepening her decline. A doctor recommended complete rest — she was not allowed to even touch a paintbrush. Nor was she fit to make the long boat trip back home. Instead, she was to take a full year off and recuperate in a sanatorium that offered generalized care for people in her situation, but specialized in tuberculosis cases. It was the worst thing he could have suggested.

Emily had lost two of her closest relatives to tuberculosis, the lung disease that was the scourge of the 19th century. Of her four brothers, only one, Richard, survived infancy only to succumb to the disease in his early 20s. Emily was devastated. Dick had been her playmate when they were little and her comfort when they were orphaned. Her beloved mother, after whom she was named, had been sick with TB for years before finally wasting away when Emily was in her early teens. Emily's memories were full of images of her mother bedridden and breathing with terrible little gasps.

Emily's grim, authoritarian father was crushed by his wife's death. He terrified his children with the mild religious mania he developed soon after, only to pass away himself a couple of years later.

Her four older sisters were left to look after Emily. Edith, Clara, Lizzie, and Alice were small-minded, religious women who were very conscious of their social position. They were horrified by their rambunctious little sister and never lost a chance to put her down. It began when they were children and continued all their lives. Emily was a dreamy, difficult child and would bite and scratch when she was displeased. Her sisters thought she was spoiled and needed to be taken down a peg or two. At times their disapproval spilled over into brutality. Her eldest sister had even beaten her with a riding whip in order to keep her in line. No one would have suspected that the sickly sweet behaviour they showed to the world masked such cruel dispositions.

Emily had chosen to sail away to England to escape her sisters, to paint, and be free. Instead, she found herself cooped up among "lung cases" who were slowly dying from the disease that had claimed the two people who were dearest to her. It was not the ideal place to recuperate from what she was ashamed to admit was a complete nervous breakdown.

Conditions at the East Anglia Sanatorium were primitive. On her first day there, Emily was surprised to find a mound of snow on her bed. Even in the dead of winter, the sanatorium windows were flung open to let in therapeutic breezes.

Nor did the medical profession have a very enlightened method of treating depression back in the early 1900s. The official diagnosis of Emily's illness was "hysteria," a catch-all term given by pre-Freudian doctors to any emotional problem suffered by a woman. No one seemed to know what to do with her. They put her in a wheelchair, which she detested, then clucked their tongues but did nothing to help her.

When she was not being neglected by the staff, Emily was subjected to a regimen of "massage, a great deal of electricity and very heavy feeding" as well as enforced bed rest. It was an experimental treatment that was extremely ineffective. It likely made Emily worse. The patients at the sanatorium were divided into "Ups" and "Downs" according to how well they were, and Emily was a near-constant "Down." The year she was meant to stay there came and went.

Emily, who loved poetry as much as she loved art, was forbidden to read her favourite books or draw in her notepad. Defying her doctor's orders, she sketched occasionally and even wrote comic poems about the staff and her fellow inmates, but it was not enough. Long, solitary walks were considered morbid and strongly discouraged, but the sanatorium was a dangerous place to make friends. Their names had a bad habit of turning up on gravestones in the local churchyard. Emily was bored and terribly unhappy and could not seem to make any progress.

To keep herself occupied, she trapped songbirds and raised the chicks with the vague notion of importing them back to Canada. They were the delight of the sanatorium. Other patients would appear at her window with little treats of bugs and worms for her new pets. It was a distraction, but it did not last. The cages made the birds anxious and they began to attack one another. At her lowest ebb, worried that she could not look after them properly, she had one of her caregivers put the birds to sleep. It seemed like everywhere she looked, she was surrounded by death.

Finally, after a year and a half in hospital, she was deemed strong enough to leave. Though she was not cured, she was well enough to travel. She puttered around England for a few more months and even resumed her studies for a while, but in June 1904 she crept home to Canada, a woman broken in spirit.

Return to Canada

Emily's five and a half years in England were meant to take her to a new level in her development. She was supposed to return to Canada sophisticated, grown-up, an artist. Instead she came back sick and humbled, but otherwise unchanged.

Her real recovery began not in the sanatorium, but after her return, when she spent some time in the Cariboo region of BC on a ranch owned by a girlhood friend. There she was briefly allowed to live out a Western fantasy. She endured a bumpy ride to the ranch, travelling from the CPR train station on a stagecoach drawn by six horses. But although she was uncomfortable, her mood lightened with every jolting step.

The Cariboo was beautiful, untamed country, and Emily was happy. What's more, she was surrounded by animals. She could ride horses, herd cattle, and shiver in her bed while coyotes howled in the night. It was heaven. She trapped chipmunks and squirrels to raise back home, perhaps thinking of those English songbirds she had loved. Her friend preferred to use them for target practice. The open spaces were a balm after the confines of the sanatorium. Emily could not get enough of this wild place.

After two months of bliss, it was back to reality. The thought of showing her face around Victoria was unappealing, but she could no longer postpone her return. Mercifully, she only had to spend a brief time in her hometown, fending off questions about her British adventure gone horribly wrong and scandalizing her sisters with several new-found bad habits, including cigarettes and the terrible social vices of card-playing and slang-filled language. Everyone remarked that England had not refined her at all. When an offer came to teach at the Ladies' Art Club in Vancouver, she jumped at the chance.

It proved to be another embarrassment. The

genteel ladies of the club — Emily actually referred to them as dames and hussies — could scarcely believe that this awkward, dowdy young woman was the London-trained artist they had heard about. They brazenly ignored her teaching plan and patronized her without mercy. "You may look at my work if you would like to, but I wish no criticism from you," one of the ladies icily informed her. She was fired within a month.

Instead of returning to Victoria with her tail between her legs, she opted to remain in Vancouver and set up her own studio. She resumed giving lessons to children, who loved her as a teacher. With her slightly immature personality, she was the perfect playmate. She also had another, more grown-up job as a political cartoonist, though it is hard to imagine a less political person. It was an ideal set-up: she could maintain her independence, yet remain fairly close to home.

The art scene in Vancouver was scarcely bigger than that in Victoria, and it was not possible for Emily to sell enough paintings to make a living, but this was still a happy time for her. She absolutely adored Stanley Park — a piece of Canadian wilderness in the heart of the city — and went on many fruitful sketching expeditions there, by herself and with her young students. She began to head out on short excursions to wilder, more remote places on her days off. It was what she had missed the whole time she was in England, where pretty little parks masqueraded as forests, and even the most uninhabited areas seemed to have an overly cultivated, cared-for look.

But she still brooded over what she perceived as her failure in London. There was so much she felt she had not accomplished. She was dissatisfied with the work she was producing, and teaching was eating into the hours she could spend painting on her own. She had been told, over and over, that the Canadian landscape was unpaintable, that Europe was the place to go to become a true artist. It was not too late. She was still young and idealistic. She'd had a few years to recover from her unpleasant experiences overseas and was intrigued by the rumblings she heard about an explosive "New Art" that was revolutionizing France. This might be just what she was looking for.

She held a tea party and charity auction in her studio, with all proceeds going straight into her travelling fund. It was not a great success. One observer even called it "pathetic." But with her meagre auction profits and the little she had saved from her teaching jobs, she was able to sail to France with Alice, the favourite of her four sisters, in July 1910.

Paris Sojourn

It was immediately obvious that Paris was going to be much more stimulating than London ever was. A young, bohemian couple, the Gibbs, took Emily under their wing and gave her a first taste of the "New Art." Although Harry Gibb was humourless and a painter of dubious talent, he had many important connections in Parisian art circles. He was a crony of Gertrude Stein, the influential poet and critic, and was a friend and colleague of many avant-garde artists of the time.

Eager to win new converts to the cause, Gibb led Emily around his studio, using his own paintings to illustrate the principles of modernism. Emily was nearly mute with excitement. The unorthodox use of colour dazzled her. She loved its "rich, delicious juiciness," so different from the timid, conventional palette she was used to. She raved that his best paintings were "brilliant, luscious, clean," but they were not all pleasing to her. She was taken aback by the more abstract and outrageous elements. Gibb's paintings of distorted nudes particularly offended her. She felt the modernist use of exaggeration and distortion was glib and empty, "designed to shock rather than convince." Her sister Alice was so appalled she could not even bring herself to look at them.

Gibb recommended she attend the Colarossi

School, unkindly suggesting that she would benefit from working alongside male artists. Though the place stank of sweat and smoke, it had an impressive pedigree: a half-dozen influential artists including Matisse. Van Gogh, a favourite of Emily's, had studied there before her. This was exactly the kind of encouragement she had been craving.

One small obstacle remained. She could not speak a word of French. Eager as always to surround herself with animals, she had purchased a parrot, Josephine, who could croak out more French words than she could. Alice, a teacher and an intelligent woman, knew the language, having learnt it specifically for the trip, but she was too stubborn and shy to serve as an interpreter and had better things to do than attend classes with her sister. Emily had to learn about the bold new French scene second-hand, from expatriate Englishmen, Scots, and New Zealanders. Despite the language barrier, she immersed herself in her work.

It soon became obvious that, as in England, Emily was pushing herself too hard. She began to get blinding headaches that made her sensitive to any sort of disturbance. She retreated to her little rented room in agony. Her old problems were beginning to resurface. By the end of the year she was back in hospital, unable to cope with the strain.

Fortunately, this episode was much less severe than her first breakdown. Though the stress of the bustling city and her workaholic tendencies were once again working against her, she did not have the tremendous social pressure that she had faced in England. There she had not been able to lift a finger without someone telling her she was doing it all wrong. French society was more permissive, especially in the somewhat unconventional circles she frequented. No one cared if she was badly dressed and carried a parrot around on her shoulder. And if anyone *did* disapprove of her, she could not understand a word they were saying.

After a short stay in Sweden to convalesce, she was back in France in the spring of 1911, ready to pick up her paintbrush once more. Since, she reasoned, her problems stemmed from overwork and the excessive stimulation of city life (though in a blatant cover-up she would later blame her illness on bronchitis, the measles, or the flu), the solution was once again to get out of the city and into the country. Leaving her sister in Paris, she journeyed first to a small town just outside of Paris, and then on to Brittany on the west coast.

Breton Landscape
Brittany in particular captivated Emily. It was the perfect blend of the gritty and the romantic, and it was

here that she started to come into her own. Being in Brittany was like travelling back in time. The Breton peasant women still wore the traditional black-and-white outfits they had since medieval times, complete with elaborate lace headdresses and heavy wooden shoes. Twenty years earlier, Paul Gauguin had come to this region and painted the most dazzling pictures of these captivating creatures, igniting the Fauvist movement, with its distorted perspective and brilliant palette. The area had consequently become an artistic hotspot and a mecca for tourists.

Emily befriended a few of the peasant women using smiles and sign language to convey her intentions. She was permitted to visit and paint their very humble homes, which she found even more shockingly poor than some of the impoverished Native settlements she had seen back home. The women were always happy to share what little they had with this smiling stranger, and Emily would never forget how stunned and happy she made a little girl one day when she twisted a couple of dirty old paint rags into a cloth doll for her. The few paintings of Emily's that remain from this time, though marked by the use of bolder colours and broad, loose brushstrokes, also have a comfortable, domestic charm as the artist was able to capture the Breton women at their most relaxed, knitting and performing other household tasks.

But it was not only the simple people of Brittany who opened their arms to Emily. The Paris art world welcomed her, too. Every year, the capital held public exhibitions featuring the best the art world had to offer. The Salon d'Automne was the "rebel Paris show" of the year, featuring the work of the most daring non-academic artists working in France. Having a painting on display at this show in the Grand Palais on the Champs Élysées would not necessarily bring fame or fortune, but the Salon was still rigorously competitive and prestigious.

With a little encouragement from Harry Gibb, Emily submitted a few of her better new canvases. To her astonishment, two of her paintings were accepted. The fact that one of her private teachers, a Scotsman named John Fergusson, was on the jury might have had something to do with her success. It was still exciting news, and proof of how much and how quickly her work had improved, especially since she had been ill and out of commission for a good portion of her stay.

Emily had of course exhibited before, in student shows, in her own studio, and with the British Columbia Society of Fine Arts. But it was one thing to show off her work with an organization she had helped to start up a few years earlier, and another to show it alongside

Europe's avant-garde elite. Emily was not at that level —
her paintings were subdued and modest compared to
the more groundbreaking works on show — but she still
had a lot to be proud of. Inclusion in the show meant
she was not just an amateur, a dabbler from the back-
waters of Canada. It meant she was, at last, a real artist.

The accolades kept coming. Harry Gibb surprised
Emily one day by making an extraordinary prediction.
He had always taken a special interest in her work, more
than in that of his other students. Emily had assumed it
was because he was impressed with her strong work
ethic, but that was not the case. Gibb, in his matter-of-
fact way, informed her that she was on her way to
becoming one of the foremost artists of her time. It was
a remarkable and inspiring comment, somewhat
diminished when he specified that he meant one of the
foremost *female* artists.

This was the sort of infuriating comment Emily
would hear again and again throughout her career. She
usually signed her paintings with her initials only and
would occasionally overhear strangers refer to "that
chap's" work, implying it was too strong to be a
woman's. She despised that attitude, particularly as she
grew older and less tolerant. It drove her wild when infe-
rior male artists patronized her. In later years she ban-
ished from her studio any male she suspected of looking

down on her because of her sex. But while she was still young and somewhat in awe of authority, she was obliged to accept such veiled insults as compliments.

Though she had made huge strides, Emily began to feel that she had absorbed all she could from her new teachers. Her time in France was winding down and money was running out. With Harry Gibb's words of praise still ringing in her ears, Emily packed up her canvases, stuck her parrot in a cage, and set sail for Canada, triumphant.

Chapter 2
Home Again

It was another grey, drizzly, BC winter, but the studio shone with the warmth of a French summer. Fresh from her success in Europe, Emily was eager to show off all she had accomplished. She would hold a public exhibition of the best pictures from her year overseas. Still a teacher at heart, she wanted to educate the people of Vancouver, show them how their tired, safe art had been made redundant, and get them talking about the new art style she had come to love.

Emily certainly got them talking, but not in the way she had hoped. The bold new style was greeted with confusion in some circles, with hostility and laughter in others. Her work was childish, bizarre, even threatening to the eyes of staid locals. The more polite would praise the frames the canvases were in. Others simply pretended not to see the paintings as they walked by, or made snide comments while she was within hearing range. Newspaper reviews were kind but bewildered and did nothing to advance her cause. It was a terrible blow. Her success in Paris had convinced her she would succeed on home soil. She faced rejection and public humiliation instead.

Her sisters begged her to go back to her old style of painting. The impressive steps she had taken in Europe were now a serious detriment. She was a disgrace to the family. Not only would she bring shame on the Carr name, but she would destroy her livelihood as well. No one in their right mind would buy these atrocious paintings or entrust this madwoman to teach their children how to draw pretty, pleasing pictures.

Emily was outraged. Though she was terribly sensitive to criticism, she was amazingly stubborn as well. Hadn't her mentor predicted she would be one of the foremost female artists of her time? There was no way she was going to turn her back on her recent victories. She had faced setbacks before and survived. This time, though, it was not her mental or physical health that was at risk, but something a little more prosaic: her finances.

The House of All Sorts

Unfortunately, her sisters' predictions came true. Sales and students were both scarce. Her main sources of revenue had dried up, and Emily was forced to move back to Victoria. The legacy left by her merchant father, roughly $50,000, was long gone, eaten up in part by her year and a half in a British hospital and by the illness and subsequent death of her brother Richard.

But her father had left land as well as money. The sisters divided up the ground that their beautiful, spacious, childhood home was situated on, and Emily received a tiny lot to do with as she pleased. In a surprisingly practical move she chose to build a small house, divided up into rental apartments. Construction began in 1913, from her own rough diagrams. She would live in a specially built flat on the premises, complete with studio, and use the rent money to finance her artistic career. It was a good plan, but Emily's plans always seemed to go awry. It was no different now.

One thing she had not counted on was World War I. Money was tight, tenants were scarce, and those who did apply were perhaps not the sort of people that Emily would have associated with if she'd had a choice.

She was creeping toward middle age, and a lifetime of hardship and disappointment had turned the high-spirited girl into an embittered and judgmental woman. She was no longer the type to joke and laugh through misfortune.

Though she might look down on her tenants, she was no prize herself. Her genteel parents would have been mortified, had they lived to see her. Her prudish, pious sisters were certainly dismayed. Her actions provoked as much scandal as her art. They ranged from mild forms of rebellion — she boasted that she was the first female in Victoria to ride a horse astride, not side-saddle — to more serious misdemeanours. Emily smoked, swore, and had a vicious side to her personality. She freely admitted she hated her tenants, who would stroll into her studio, mock her paintings, and trouble her with a variety of complaints. Their increasing demands and criticisms drove her wild, and she was not afraid to retaliate.

Emily had always been scrappy, a fighter, but now she was becoming tough and ruthless. She did not have any time for her tenants' sob stories. They either behaved themselves and paid their rent on time, or they were kicked out. One woman, a widow, was in dire financial straits and had been selling off her expensive furniture piece by piece. Emily was already sour on her:

the widow would rattle the entire house with her piano-playing and the resounding slaps she gave her young son. When her tenant tried to trade an old stove for a month's rent, Emily was incensed. She snatched a basket of pots and pans belonging to the other woman and held them for ransom, telling her tenant she would get them back once she had coughed up the rent money. The woman tore upstairs to Emily's apartment and screamed and swore at her. Emily had had enough. She grabbed a dirty metal bucket from the basket and slammed it over the widow's head. The woman staggered down the stairs to her apartment, wearing the bucket like a hat. Emily laughed. She felt the law was on her side and was unrepentant.

This was not an isolated incident. There were more violent encounters. One tenant punched Emily in the face when she refused to call a plumber over a broken tap (she eventually subdued him with a squirt of water from the garden hose). She deliberately broke the glasses of another man when she caught him trying to turn up the heat, then narrowly averted a brawl with him. Encounters like these became a regular occurrence. She was not the genteel creature she'd been brought up to be.

She seemed to be spending more time with lawyers and the police than with friends and family. She did not just want peace and quiet. She wanted revenge. When she was especially frustrated she would unplug the fuses and turn off the water, just to torture her boarders.

The apartment was first named Hill House, though later Emily called it the House of All Sorts — and she certainly did get all sorts. She was plagued by drunks, drug addicts, con artists, and, most horribly in Emily's eyes, unwed couples. Being a landlady meant being a maid, a cook, a doctor, a jack-of-all-trades. Though she soon realized she was not cut out to do the job, the poor state of the economy meant she was unable to sell the building. She was forced to reduce the rent she charged and as a result was only earning a fraction of what she had expected.

The spacious apartments were eventually divided up into boarding rooms, and the quality of tenant somehow declined even further. Emily's studio was turned into a common room for her boarders. When times were especially tough, she rented out her own apartment and slept in a tent in the garden or in a storage room in the basement.

Despite these problems, Emily threw herself into her role as landlady. Always somewhat immature for her age, she set out to prove to her sisters that she was not a silly, flighty, impractical girl, but a responsible woman. She cooked meals, painted walls, took care of the plumbing and heating, and scoured the place from top to bottom. She even did minor carpentry work around the house. She did her own baking, made her own soap, sewed her clothes, stretched her own canvases, and built her own easels. At one point she tore up the garden fence to make picture frames.

The creative energy Emily used to expend on her art was now being spent finding new ways to make and save money. She hooked rugs that were beautiful enough to hang on the walls, and she designed ornamental ceramics with motifs drawn from Northwest Coast Native art. This was no small undertaking. She would march down to the local cliffs with shovel in hand to dig out the clay herself. Then she beat the impurities out of it and hand-fashioned the clay into a variety of small objects: bowls, ashtrays, candlesticks, and the like. She fired up to 500 of these small pieces at a time, facing the scorching heat (and fire hazard) of her backyard kiln. After hand-painting and glazing each one, she sold them in local tourist shops and at craft fairs all around Canada. They were cheap and lopsided and had a tendency to break, but were made with a great deal of flare, and tourists snapped them up by the dozen.

Most of her other money-making schemes did not involve her artistic talents. She raised rabbits and chickens and sold produce from her garden. Even by wartime standards, she was amazingly frugal and hard-working.

The Menagerie

Despite the non-stop drudgery, money remained a problem. A lifelong dog lover — when she was a child, her very first drawing was a charcoal sketch of a dog, scribbled on the back of a brown paper bag — Emily now started rearing purebreds for profit. First there were sheepdogs, around 350 of them over the space of four years, and then, possibly due to space constraints, scruffy little griffons.

She gave the sheepdogs silly, affectionate nicknames like Punk and Lady Loo, or dignified biblical names, such as Adam and Eve and Moses. There was a kennel in the backyard, a special "puppy room" for newborns in the basement, and a canine graveyard in the backyard. One year a viral illness, distemper, broke out among the sheepdogs and killed all but three of the puppies. Emily was forced to drown the sickliest ones in a bucket. Despite minor tragedies such as this, her prize-winning animals provided a much-needed source of income in these hard times, and gave her companionship as well. From then on she was never without a dog (or three or four) by her side.

Being at the beck and call of her tenants left Emily little time to explore nature as she loved to do.

Gradually, to compensate, she began to bring nature, more specifcally animals, indoors. It started with the dogs. Then it was cats, rats, raccoons, squirrels, and any wild animal she could tame. She was always fond of birds; besides owning the usual parrots and canaries, she once owned a pet vulture. There was a succession of white rats, who would play hide-and-seek in her clothing and terrify the life out of her sisters. If elephants had been native to BC, she would have owned a herd of them. One of her great regrets in life was that she never owned a baboon.

Eventually, Emily traded one of her purebred puppies for a real prize: a little Javanese monkey with greyish fur and slanted, haunting eyes. Emily named her Woo in imitation of the crooning call she made. Her sisters were naturally aghast, but Emily treated Woo like the daughter she never had. Woo was no baboon, but Emily worshipped her all the same. She dressed the monkey in frilly red dresses, played "This Little Piggy" on her toes, spanked her when she was naughty, and filled up a stocking full of treats for her at Christmas time. Emily even taught Woo how to sew. She spent hours passing a needle through a piece of scrap material, though she never learned how to manage the thread.

Woo spent some of her time locked up in a parrot cage, but she was occasionally allowed to roam through the house. Dinner guests were alarmed to see that Woo had free rein in the kitchen, where she would curl up in the stove when it was turned off. In the summer, Woo lived in a box high in a tree in the backyard and would amuse herself trying to pluck clothespins from the clothesline. Emily, who painted few portraits, immortalized Woo twice on canvas, once depicting her as a savage beast peering out of the trees, once as a fetching little miss in a pinafore.

But Woo was still at heart a wild animal and would bite or scratch when irritated. She was only partially housetrained, and on one occasion relieved herself in Emily's shoe. There were a few near-death experiences thanks to her habit of scattering tubes of paint on the floor, then eating the colour that caught her eye. Green and yellow were her favourites. Emily had to force emetics down the monkey's throat during a couple of tense midnight vigils.

A Sunday Painter
What with caring for her tenants and her ever-increasing menagerie, Emily had little free time to herself. Though she never fully abandoned painting, as myth would have it, her day-to-day worries slowly smothered her artistic intentions. The woman who had nearly sacrificed her mental health for the sake of her ambitions

Emily Carr ca. 1936 with one of her oil paintings

had become a "Sunday painter" — painting a little on the side, but as a hobby only. She rarely bothered to exhibit her work, which was still way ahead of its time in comparison to that of other Victoria artists. She no longer made money from her art, and money was her top priority.

People in Victoria gradually forgot Emily as an artist, though they all knew her by sight. She had always been unconcerned about how she appeared to others. As a student she used to sport an enormous tam-o'-shanter that looked like a plaid pillow balanced on her head. A few years later, when she was still teaching art to youngsters, she had startled one student who stumbled upon her crouched on all fours, wearing her old-fashioned bathing suit and scrubbing the studio floor.

Her fashion sense had not improved over the years, and age and illness had eroded her good looks. She now wore a series of severe black homemade dresses, mass-produced on a sewing machine she bought on layaway. These covered an increasingly chunky frame — juice fasts and fad diets had little effect on her slow and steady weight gain. On her head she wore a distinctive skullcap that became her trademark, or a shapeless and unfashionable black hat. Wire-framed granny glasses and the most comfortable, durable, and hideous of shoes completed the look.

People began to whisper. Emily Carr was "queer and loony." She would walk around with her pet monkey on a chain, like a dog. On shopping days she would strap a saddle onto a sheepdog and use it as a packhorse, or trundle around a wicker baby carriage in lieu of a shopping cart. She was quite a head-turner. Much about her appearance could be attributed to a mix of poverty, practicality, and a purposeful defiance of social norms. But for all intents and purposes, Emily Carr had turned into a crackpot.

Looking for a "Soul Pal"

Emily was much more sensitive to animals than she ever was to humans. Whenever she served her tenants fish for supper, she removed the fishbowl from the dining area so the goldfish would not be traumatized. She would never have indulged any person to that degree. Her journals are filled with longings for a "soul pal," but her paranoid streak made her doubt the sincerity of the friendships she did have. She'd always had a jealous nature and had provoked rivalries among her sisters when she was little, behaviour she never quite grew out of. As an adult, she could be very unpleasant when crossed, and not only to her tenants.

Emily was extremely anti-social in an age when formal visits and letters of introduction were still the norm.

She kept the chairs in her studio suspended from the ceiling on a pulley system, ostensibly to save room, but really to discourage unwanted visitors. She was not always that subtle. One wrong word and those visitors might find themselves out on the street, a string of abuse ringing in their ears. She drove many people out of her life in this way. Most of her companions were younger; it took a lot of energy to be Emily's friend. Letters had to be answered promptly and visits made regularly or they could find themselves abruptly cut out of her life. Anything could set her off. She once provoked a vicious quarrel with her long-suffering friend Edythe Hembroff over how spoons should be arranged in the cutlery drawer.

Her love life was non-existent, though it was not always that way. A great beauty in her younger years, with her slanted, feline eyes and flirtatious manner, Emily had managed to attract the attention of several admirers and had fallen passionately in love exactly once. She would dreamily recall the sensation of rubbing her cheek against the rough tweed of his jacket, and the single kiss they shared. She was terribly embarrassed when she found out she meant nothing to him, and she never revealed his name.

A more down-to-earth lover was William "Mayo" Paddon, a ship's purser she met on a trip up the coast when she was in her late 20s. Four years younger than she was and extremely religious, Mayo rigorously pursued Emily long after she lost interest. They would attend church together and hold hands, go for long walks and discuss scripture. It was Mayo who had followed Emily to England, begging her to abandon art and become his wife. "Come home, Emily; marry me; you do not belong here," he sighed. At one point he was proposing to her on average five times a week, but she sensibly decided that marriage without love, at least on her part, would make her miserable.

Emily might have enjoyed the attention, but after a while Mayo became a nuisance. He would literally pray that she would change her mind and marry him. They lost touch after her final, decisive rejection, and he married another woman soon after. Following a chance encounter in San Francisco a decade and a half after their romance ended, he took to sending her a single pressed flower every year at Christmas. He kept a sprig of heather that they had collected on a woodland walk pressed between the pages of his Bible; it was still there when he died. Emily had made quite an impression on his heart. He never got over his love for her.

Though Emily disliked humanity as a whole, she had several good reasons to be particularly unenthusiastic about the opposite sex. For one, she lived in a rampantly sexist era, when women were mostly denied any opportunities other than marriage and motherhood. Emily and her sisters were also raised to believe that men were simply better than women. Their mother flatly stated that men were put on earth to be worshipped by women, but Emily never quite believed it. The main reason she found men so distasteful was because of her father and an episode she would later refer to, rather melodramatically, as "the brutal telling."

The Brutal Telling

Richard Carr was a firm, authoritarian figure; some might call him a despot and a bully. There's no doubt that he dominated his sickly, much younger wife and that he used the Bible and the silent treatment to intimidate his children — even Emily, his special favourite.

Carr was the classic self-made man. He had sailed from England as a young man, seeking, in the time-honoured fashion, to make his fortune. He did it selling groceries to gold miners during the California gold rush, and with his new-found wealth he settled in Victoria, the most English town in North America, to raise his ever-expanding brood in an approximation of the British fashion.

He and Emily were not terribly dissimilar. In his youth, he had been a wanderer and an amateur photographer, loved the great outdoors, wrote devotedly in his journal, was maybe even a bit of a dreamer. However, by the time Emily, the eighth of nine children, was born, he was in late middle age and had turned strict, sour, and pious. Neighbourhood children would flee from his path; his own children could never please him. Emily suspected that he loved his garden more than he loved his own wife.

Carr was a difficult man, but up until her adolescence she had always respected him. She liked to look back on her childhood as an idyllic time when the world was a children's picture book brought to life, and sweet young things frolicked with ponies and ducklings and flowers, all under the watchful but loving eyes of their angelic mother. Then, suddenly, it all went horribly wrong.

Though she would never give details about the "telling," and in fact kept it a secret till a few years before her death, it seems her father explained the facts of life to Emily in an extremely explicit way. He may have attempted to give her a practical demonstration as well. He might also have revealed that her mother, whom she regarded as a near-saintly figure, was in fact an illegitimate child, a social taboo in those times.

In any event, Emily felt a black cloud had passed over her previously happy childhood, and she was reduced to "agonies of terror" from then on whenever she was in the presence of the man she now thought of as a repulsive old hypocrite. Needless to say, she rapidly fell from her position as his favoured child. She felt more betrayed than sad when he died: though she was still a minor, he omitted any reference to her in his will and left her in the care of her hated eldest sister, Edith, a carbon copy of their abusive father.

Whatever the specifics of the incident, the result was an almost pathological prudery, even by Victorian standards. When she was first offered the chance to take a Life class at the San Francisco art school, she refused and rather grandly proclaimed, "I will never draw from the nude." Though she later relented, she preferred female models — the agony of viewing a naked male form was just too much for her. At the Colarossi School in Paris, she became so agitated at the sight of male flesh that she quickly switched to classes with draped models. She went into a frenzy when an acquaintance told her he saw "erotic symbolism" in her work. She hated the modern trend of explicit sex in art and literature — "muck" is how she termed it.

It is likely that Emily never had a lover. After her death, however, a friend and former tenant, Philip Amsden, claimed that the two of them had lived together in a rented cottage one summer. If it was true, it was probably more of a practical arrangement than a romantic one — Emily spent most of her time sketching.

As a landlady, Emily kept an eye out for any sign that couples boarding with her were living in sin. She would evict them without a second thought if her suspicions proved to be true. Married couples also came under her scrutiny. She was mortified when one slovenly young housewife let her underthings air-dry in the front window of the apartment house.

Though she had four sisters and had lived communally in dorms and boarding houses when she was a student, she was excessively modest, even around other women. On a sketching trip with her friend Edythe Hembroff, also an artist, she made the other woman turn away and swear not to peek while she hastily slipped into her nightie. This behaviour was very odd, considering how cheerfully she would defy social convention in many other ways. The woman who loved to shock others was quite easily shocked herself.

This was just one of the many contradictory facets of Emily's personality. She was the devoted artist who abandoned her calling; the nature lover who was tied to her home; the passionate young girl who became the asexual woman. And despite all her attention-seeking behaviour, someone who carries a live rat in her front pocket probably does not want others to get too close.

But Emily, who liked to see herself as the consummate loner, also had a slowly growing network of influential friends and supporters, thanks to a hobby that started on a pleasure trip to Alaska back in 1907.

Chapter 3
The Laughing One

Growing up in Victoria in the late 1800s, Emily was hardly a poster child for multiculturalism. Though roughly half the city was made up of Native peoples, Emily, the pampered daughter of a well-to-do family, had very little contact with any non-European culture. There were the Chinese servants, of course, helped out by the quiet woman who wore her long black hair in braids and came to do the laundry once a week, a Native woman known as Wash Mary. Emily also spotted the occasional elaborately carved canoe docked in the bay, carrying Native families on excursions down the coast, and the

Songhees village could just about be seen across the harbour.

That was as close as she was allowed to get. Under no circumstances would there be any socializing with these people. White, middle-class society viewed them with a mixture of pity and contempt. The only time Emily was permitted to enter Wash Mary's home was on a sympathy call when the woman was on her deathbed. Emily's own father, not known for his generous nature, surprised everyone one day by handing out free raisins from his shop to a group of Native people. He later explained that the raisins were infested with maggots — not good enough to sell to whites, but certainly good enough for a bunch of Indians.

Emily herself claimed to hate just two types of people: missionaries and the English. Ironically, it was the former who gave Emily her first real contact with Native life. In 1899, just prior to her departure for England, she was invited on an expedition to Ucluelet, on the west coast of Vancouver Island, by a missionary friend of her pious sister Lizzie. The town was isolated, had been devastated by the decimation of the sealing industry, and was plagued by disease and alcohol abuse. The inhabitants survived on a diet of fish, fish, and more fish, and on the tiny amount of money earned from the sale of the mats they wove.

The Laughing One

Emily's interest in Native culture was piqued despite the terrible squalor. She liked and respected the Native people far more than she did her hosts, the missionaries. She could not stand the way they would herd the adults of the village into the tiny schoolroom in order to preach at them as if they were children. She did admire their tenacity, though: the missionaries had failed to convert a single person in all the years they had been installed in the town.

Emily was inspired by the village's magnificent setting. Though she was too daunted by the majesty of the surrounding rain forest to attempt to paint it, she used hand gestures and a friendly smile to gain permission to sketch the Nootka villagers and their driftwood houses. It was the same method she would use a few years later in France to communicate with the peasant women of Brittany, and it earned her a nickname: Klee Wyck or "The Laughing One."

Fascinated by Native culture, Emily made casual sketching trips to Native villages whenever she could, but it was not until 1907 that she accidentally found her calling. That year, Emily and her sister Alice travelled by boat and train up to Alaska, passing through the ghost towns and debris left by the Klondike gold rush. It was in the northern villages that she saw her first totem poles — and her first example of how *not* to paint them.

The little island town of Sitka was tailored toward inquisitive European travellers. One could purchase a more-or-less authentic tom-tom or a festively coloured basket, then take a stroll down to Totem Walk, where Haida and Tlingit totem poles, uprooted from their original locations, had been slapped with a few garish coats of paint and then replanted in a tidy row for curious tourists to admire. Afterward, a trip to Mr. Theodore J. Richardson's studio might be in order. There visitors could purchase scenic paintings, with totem poles sticking up like candy canes in the middle of the landscape. Emily thought they looked tacked on, like a "cherry on the top of a cake."

It is hard to say if Emily was more inspired or offended by what she saw. Whatever her emotion, she proceeded to hatch an astonishingly ambitious plan.

Though Emily was no scholar, she realized that if traditional Native culture was being slowly destroyed, so too were the monumental wooden carvings she admired. Museums and collectors had snapped up the finest specimens, leaving the rest to rot. Among the Native peoples, the old skills were being forgotten; there would be few carvers to replace the ones who were gone.

She decided she would track down as many totem poles as possible in their original settings. She would

have to study and research the symbols, and then produce worthy and accurate likenesses of these huge,
complex works. And she would do all this in spite of
being a chubby little lady with a limited income, who
suffered from poor health.

It would not be easy. The totems were now only to
be found in the more inaccessible villages around the
province. She would have to hire guides, sail and trek to
remote spots in northern BC and throughout the Queen
Charlotte Islands, then make camp or hire a room for a
dollar or so a night. As always, there was the language
barrier, and the cash problem. Expenses might mount
as high as $10 or more a day, a largish sum for the time
and a steep price for someone who was often living
hand to mouth.

In June 1908, at the age of 36, Emily embarked on
her first major sketching trip, travelling to Alert Bay off
the north coast of Vancouver Island. Emily left only hazy
verbal accounts of those summertime trips, which
numbered in the dozens, but her sketches speak
volumes about the beauty and isolation of the places
she visited. "To reach the villages was difficult," she
noted, "and accommodation a serious problem," but
the stunning work she was beginning to produce made
it all worthwhile.

For the most part there was more discomfort than

danger. Emily, prone to violent seasickness, endured rickety boats, the muggy summer heat, and strong rains that could dissolve charcoal and ruin paint and paper. It was sometimes so damp that matches would not light, leaving her with no fire to dry her clothes or keep her warm through the night. Then there were the ever-present clouds of mosquitoes. To protect herself from them she wore her "mosquito armour," which consisted of long pants worn under her usual black dress, two pairs of gloves, and a heavy veil with a little window in front to peer through.

There was a mild risk of attack by the feral, half-starved dogs that sometimes prowled the villages, but her own dog was usually tough enough to scare them off. A particularly ferocious cur with a face full of porcupine quills became as sweet as a puppy after she had fed it and plucked its face clean.

No, the wild dogs weren't the problem. It was the larger, predatory animals she'd been warned about, particularly bears and cougars, that made her nervous. Her canine companion of the moment, Billie the mutt or Ginger Pop the griffon, would not be much protection against such predators — they would be the appetizer. But her fears were unfounded. The only time she was ever attacked was when she entered one otherwise empty village only to be set upon by a pack of purring domestic cats rubbing affectionately up against her legs. The villages themselves were eerie places. Whole populations had been decimated by smallpox or had fled south to an easier life. She might arrive at a desolate fishing village only to find it abandoned for the season. Sometimes a few old or sickly inhabitants lingered, left behind by the rest of their people, who had trickled down to the canneries or the cities.

The dramatically carved totems could be disturbing in their own way. Some of them were funerary poles with wooden coffins perched on top. Old bones could sometimes be seen spilling out of the coffins. Emily did not consider herself to be particularly superstitious, though the menacing silence of the forest could incite an overactive imagination. During one thunderstorm, while she sought shelter under a covered burial site, her foot knocked against a rattle that was planted on the ground. She fled in terror when she realized she was standing on a shaman's grave, absurd thoughts of black magic racing through her head.

Some of the carvings were purposely menacing. Emily was dumbstruck by the imposing cedar wood carving that stood guard in several villages, a wild-eyed female figure with a gaping mouth, eagle heads for breasts, and a sea serpent draped across her forehead. This was D'Sonoqua or Zunoqua, the "wild woman of the forest," a cannibal spirit with a taste for small children. Emily was haunted by the sight of her. "The fierce wooden image often came to me," she said, "both in my waking and in my sleeping."

With no one to maintain them, the poles were often in dire condition. Insects and damp rot gradually eroded the wood. The carved images were sometimes too rotten to decipher. The lush forest would also try to reclaim its own: the poles might be half-smothered in vines, leaves, and moss. Deep in the heart of the forest, Emily stumbled across a magnificent bear carving that was surrounded by such dense growth she could not circle around to see the front of it. She settled for making a drawing of its rather fetching backside instead.

One trip was particularly dramatic. It had started unpleasantly, as the totems she wanted to paint were located near a thriving village where the locals were hostile. In some cases the residents had physically assaulted outsiders if they dared to come into town. Emily was treated coldly but not violently, did some unsatisfactory work, and was glad to get away.

Perhaps to erase this unpleasant incident from her mind, she hired a guide to take her in his gas-powered boat to revisit some of her favourite spots, the villages of Skedans, Tanoo, and Cumshewa. She paid $50 for a four-day tour. They set off on a Wednesday morning with the man's niece and nephew for company. The weather was rough, and after Emily and the girl had been put ashore, the boat's propeller became tangled in seaweed. The heaving waves caused it to surge dangerously close to a nearby reef with her guide, his nephew, and Emily's dog Ginger Pop still on board. Man and boy somehow managed to paddle to safety using the on-board canoe, leaving the dog on the drifting vessel.

The four humans were stranded on shore. While her guide mourned the possible loss of his boat, Emily mourned the possible loss of her beloved pup. They spent a wet, rough night camped on the beach, barely able to sleep due to the noise of the rain and the crashing surf.

Morning came, but their ordeal was not over yet. Though they were near fishing waters, they had difficulty flagging down passing boats. The guide suspected it was because no one wanted to help Native peoples in distress. They waited and waited until finally a Norwegian trawler came to their assistance. Emily halfwished it had not. The sea was still churning, and her ghastly seasickness was bound to erupt. It did, with a vengeance. After a few minutes on board she was sick "beyond decency." She mercifully passed out a short time later.

Around midnight she was dumped from the

Norwegian trawler onto a Japanese fishing boat and had a joyous though somewhat damp reunion with the bedraggled Ginger Pop, who had been towed to safety behind her. From there she was transferred to a small cabin on the shore of Cumshewa Inlet. She had a few hours to catch her breath before another Japanese boat arrived to scoop her up. She finally landed, nauseous, exhausted, and stinking of fish and worse, on the wharf of a nearby cannery, where she could hire transportation back to civilization. Fifty dollars she could ill afford was wasted on what amounted to a whirlwind tour of international fishing boats. Her only regret? That she had not managed to get any sketching done.

The physical difficulties of getting to the totem pole sites were not the only hurdles. From an artistic point of view, totems were not that easy to render. This was not the quaint folk art of a backward people, as some liked to believe. The Haida in particular had produced master craftsmen whose artistic skills were sought out by other tribes. They were the anonymous masters who captured the complexity of clan crests and tribal myths. It was sometimes difficult or impossible for an outsider to interpret the meaning behind the supernatural images they had portrayed.

On a technical level, their great height and decayed state made the poles a challenge to represent on paper.

Emily publicly scorned the photographers who could simply point and shoot and record what took her days, months, even years to reproduce. They could not capture the soul of the things, she said, and "ten million cameras" would never capture the "real Canada." She neglected to mention that she occasionally worked from photographs herself, when her sketches proved inadequate.

Recording the totem poles was a passion for Emily, not a mercenary venture. Most people found the resulting paintings "weird" and viewed her hobby as another example of her increasing eccentricity. When she did exhibit, she found her paintings hidden off to the side where no one would see them. Often she found her work hung high, just below the ceiling, where decent citizens need not be exposed to it. Needless to say, the totem pole paintings never sold. The result was a serious strain on her pocketbook.

There were ethical problems as well. Emily was conscious that a white woman tinkering with Native culture was open to accusations of exploitation. One of her great shames was when she began making ceramics decorated with stylized Native designs for the tourist market, for the people of the Northwest Coast were not pottery makers, but weavers and basket-makers. She assuaged her guilt somewhat by making sure the designs were ultra-authentic, carefully copying images of ravens and bears and whales from books on Native art borrowed from the library of the Provincial Museum.

Once, a haughty English "expert," who was to speak on the lives of the West Coast Native peoples, asked to borrow several of Emily's Alert Bay sketches to illustrate her talk. Emily flatly refused, distrusting the woman's motivations. The offer of free publicity and the chance to make a little money were no temptation. Emily claimed she was not working for profit, but for the sake of history.

Much of Emily's own early knowledge of Native culture had come from idealized literature, which trotted forth the old notion of the "noble savage." However, the more she immersed herself in her hobby the more she became obsessed with authenticity. It was one thing to look up D'Sonoqua's name in a worn-out reference book, quite another to see the fear in the eyes of those who still had a lingering belief in her.

It was from the connections she made with her Native guides and hosts that Emily learned the most about their culture. She went to the Esquimault reserve to attend a potlatch, the communal gift-giving ceremony that was outlawed for years by the government in an effort to wipe out Native culture. She heard traditional songs being sung and witnessed old customs being carried out. Usually very thrifty, she willingly gave away a silk blouse of hers to a dying woman who needed some proof of wealth in the next world. It began to dawn on her that these people had a life beyond what she had read about in books.

Her most helpful guides in the early days were a Haida couple named Clara and William Russ. They lived in a fairly modern house, with a front parlour and a player piano, and spoke excellent English. After they led Emily to the abandoned village she was headed for, when night had fallen and the campfire sparked, they began to entertain Emily with what she called ghost stories. These tales of spirits and the supernatural had been passed down from generation to generation and were now only half-remembered myths. But these weren't just campfire tales. Clara and William would not stay long in any place they suspected might be haunted.

Emily discovered through them that there was not just one Native experience, that these were a people balanced on the edge of modernity and tradition. This lesson was brought home by one of her most profound and long-lasting friendships.

Sophie Frank, a Squamish woman from North Vancouver, would paddle across Burrard Inlet and sell her beautiful woven cedar baskets door to door in Vancouver, where Emily was living and teaching at the time. One day Sophie knocked on her door. Emily was intrigued by this quiet, sad-eyed woman and very interested in the baskets, but she was strapped for cash as always. She did not even have any cast-off clothes to give in exchange, though she definitely had time for a chat and a smoke. Sophie was moved by her kindness and gave her a basket anyway, telling her she could wait a month for payment. The month went by, the two women met again, and when Emily made the promised payment, a solid friendship was forged.

Emily, whose relationships with others were often marred by rivalry and pettiness, was surprisingly relaxed and undemanding in her friendship with Sophie. The two would sit together, smoking and not saying much, but companionable in their silence. Sometimes Emily would visit Sophie's Salish village on the northern shore of Burrard Inlet. The two of them attended church and visited the graves of Sophie's dead children — 21 in all. Sophie named one of her little girls after Emily who, in a bizarre homage, named one of her pet rats after her old friend.

Emily, with her tendency to romanticize, liked to view Sophie as an example of the pure and simple Native soul. Sophie's motto, no matter what the circumstance, was "Nice ladies always do." Emily was shocked when she found out that her friend was in fact an alcoholic and an occasional prostitute. Though initially appalled, Emily decided, with uncharacteristic generosity, that the friendship was worth maintaining. The two remained friends for many years.

Emily's sketches of totem poles and Native villages were truly her life's work. Over the years, she took dozens of trips up the coast, made hundreds of sketches, and forged countless friendships. She journeyed by canoe and fishing boat, on foot and by train, and camped out in tents and log cabins, toolsheds and lighthouses. Eventually, the tough conditions overwhelmed her. She began to turn her attention to more accessible spots, nearer home, and to paint simple undemanding nature scenes as she had when she was a young girl. By 1927, her grand plan of recording all the totems left in BC had been abandoned. The dream was over.

* * *

Emily held the receiver to her ear, a little confused and embarrassed. The man on the phone identified himself as Eric Brown, director of the National Gallery in Ontario, and he wished to speak to Emily Carr, the artist. Up until a few minutes ago she had not been aware that Canada even *had* a National Gallery, and as far as she was concerned, Emily Carr, the artist, no longer existed. She was a landlady and an entrepreneur, and had been for years. Painting was now purely a hobby.

She was beginning to get irritated, but the gentleman on the other end was equally insistent. A government anthropologist had heard countless stories from the coastal Native peoples about a strange little woman who went around BC painting totem poles. The anthropologist had passed the information on to Brown, who was desperate to speak to her.

After years of neglect, the Gallery was turning its attention to the art of the West. Brown was planning an exhibition for the autumn that would focus on the artists and artisans of the Northwest Coast. It would be a daring mixture of traditional Native arts and modern interpretations. Fine art and ancient artifacts would hang side by side. Brown sensed that the works of Miss Emily Carr would bridge the gap between the two. He was so certain, in fact, that he had travelled by rail from Ottawa all the way to Victoria to visit her and view her work. He dangled the promise of a free round-trip railway pass out East if he liked what he saw. Would he be able to drop by her studio to view her paintings?

Eric Brown was clearly an important man, and very persuasive. She could say no, and that would be the end of it. Her life would continue as it had for years. Say yes, and she would enter the unknown. She'd had years of scorn and rejection and did not know if she could take any more.

But in the end it was an obvious choice. Emily hesitated and then, grudgingly, agreed.

Chapter 4
Rebirth

Emily should have known it would be a disaster.

It had taken hundreds of hours and thousands of dollars to pull it all together. Every last detail was attended to. Expectations had run high beforehand. Rumour had it that it was going to be one of the National Gallery's most successful shows ever. A typical opening at the Gallery could draw up to 2,000 guests, and this breakthrough exhibition, the first to showcase Canada's Western artists, was sure to be one of the most exciting ever. December 5, 1927, would go down in the Gallery's history. At a dinner before the show, Emily and the show's organizers uncorked a bottle of wine and drank a toast to their certain success. By the end of the night, they probably wished they had saved that bottle.

All dolled up in a black satin gown with elbow-length gloves, Emily stood in contrast to the works hanging on the walls behind her. In room after room there were carved and painted wooden masks and sculptures representing the myths of the Northwest Coast people. The Gallery had even brought in an authentic Native canoe. Hanging alongside were stunning modernistic landscape paintings by men with names like Varley, Jackson, and Harris. The juxtaposition was striking, original.

Interspersed between them was a selection of 27 watercolours and 11 oils by the standout artist of the evening, Emily Carr. Her dramatic portrayals of Native life and culture were the highlight of the show. Eric Brown, director of the National Gallery, was delighted by the work of this artist he proudly claimed to have discovered. Hooked rugs, which until recently had been scattered around her studio floor, were hung on the walls like artwork, and examples of the slightly crooked, highly commercial pottery that had caused her so much shame were spotlighted as well. Emily had even been commissioned to design the cover of the exhibit's catalogue, decorating it with a stylized, stiff-winged raven. She modestly signed it with her Chinook nickname, Klee Wyck.

In theory, it was vindication for all the years she had been shunned as an artist, but there was an unbelievable amount of pressure as well. Emily was jittery, pulling those fancy gloves on and off. All eyes were going to be on her. She had never experienced anything like this kind of attention before. Her success at the Salon d'Automne in Paris nearly two decades before paled in comparison.

But the expected crowds never arrived. The evening would no doubt have been a smashing success — if the organizers had remembered to send out invitations to the public and Gallery members. Instead, the handful of guests wandering around the echoing rooms at the opening party were artists and Gallery staff. As well, Emily discovered that half of the paintings she had sent were still in packing crates in the Gallery basement. A "fizzle" was how she would later describe the whole affair. The press was enthusiastic, but no interest would be generated among the public without the buzz of a successful opening night, and the show would probably close early.

Just a few months before, the show's failure would have been enough to crush her. It was true that she was nervous and eager to get away, but it was not to escape the embarrassment caused by the show's low turnout. Instead, she was anxious to return to Toronto, where she had spent a few short but fulfilling days before arriving in Ottawa. There, the painter who had faced years of rejection and isolation had finally found what she was looking for: acceptance among her artistic equals.

Emily and the Group of Seven

Emily took a stubbornly anti-intellectual stance toward her art. Simplicity, sincerity, and spirituality were the qualities she valued most in painting. She was naturally suspicious of art theory, which ran counter to her ideals. When Eric Brown suggested she prepare for her journey out East by reading a dry little tome entitled *A Canadian Art Movement* by Fred Housser, she was polite but unenthusiastic — until Brown mentioned it dealt with a Canadian version of the "New Art" that had inspired her trip to France.

Housser wrote about the Group of Seven, a collective whose work defined the current Canadian art scene. The Group's members were the most important artists Canada had ever produced, but Emily had never heard of them. She was stunned to discover that the artistic experiments that had caused her to be scorned and isolated in the West were being hailed in the East as important, groundbreaking steps in establishing a Canadian national identity. She read the book from cover to cover, carefully copying out noteworthy passages. The few reproductions of the Group's paintings looked absolutely ravishing as well. It was like discovering a whole new world.

Being the feature artist at a major show gave Emily an automatic entry into Eastern artistic circles. This meant a social whirlwind of tea parties and luncheons while she explored Toronto, Ottawa, and Montreal. More excitingly, it gave her the chance to meet most of the men responsible for the art movement she had only just found out about.

She was thrilled to be invited to visit members of the Group of Seven in their studios. She was impressed by the beauty and vision of their work, by the common goals they shared despite the differences in their personal styles, and by the kindness and generosity they showered on her — for the most part. A. Y. Jackson she found to be one of those tiresome men who looked down on women artists. Her resentment of him was based on professional jealousy, too. "I felt a little as if beaten at my own game," she confessed when she saw his Native paintings, though later she was more critical. Emily claimed he did not "feel" the West and that he "patronized feminine painting," but she likely also felt he was encroaching on her territory. With all the other men she felt an immediate emotional and artistic connection.

Emily was ecstatic. She had spent her youth travelling to Paris and London looking for some kind of direction, only to find it in mid-life in the art of her Canadian contemporaries. She visited a Group of Seven show at the Royal Canadian Academy in Montreal, a city she detested, and spent ages gazing at *Mountain Forms* by Lawren Harris. It moved her more than any painting she had ever seen before. She was furious when she overheard some women mocking it, saying that it resembled an angel food cake. It reinforced the bond she felt with him, however, as she had faced the same treatment herself many times in the past.

Of all the people she met on her Eastern journey, it was Harris who was to have the most influence on her life and work. She felt his landscapes had a spiritual quality lacking in the work of other painters. Her own decades-old "modernity" looked feeble in comparison to his crisp, contemporary work. They became close friends almost immediately, with a touch of hero-worship on her part. She spent a delirious evening at his home, looking at his art collection and listening to classical music on the phonograph, a revelation in itself — Emily would not even have a radio for years to come.

It was all very thrilling, and more than enough to

compensate for the failure of the West Coast art exhibit. Even that had not been a total disaster. The Gallery had purchased three of her watercolours to be kept in its permanent collection. It was quite an honour. And before she left, Harris had her make a vow that she would resume painting seriously again. They would write to each other, and he would advise and encourage her when she felt she was in need of guidance and support. "You are one of us," he later told her, to her delight.

Emily felt energized, rejuvenated. Art was no longer a lonely pursuit, but a common goal she shared with the most supportive, stimulating people she had ever encountered. But now, the West beckoned. It was time to put aside all the petty concerns of daily life and become a painter once again.

Back to Life

It would have been a magnificent gesture if, upon her return to Victoria in late December that same year, Emily had marched into the House of All Sorts and told her tenants to go to the devil. She still needed their money, however, so she settled for reclaiming her studio, which had been converted into a dining/living room for her boarders' use, and resuming her once-frequent painting expeditions.

She resurrected her old totem sketches, hundreds

of them, that had been stored in boxes in the basement, and re-examined them with a critical eye. Her exposure to the Group of Seven's work made them look flat and uninspired, but there was a wealth of source material there. She began reworking them, toning down the bright pastel colours and retooling the composition, giving them a powerful, brooding look they had lacked before.

She expanded her working relationship with a group of Seattle-area artists she had encountered, men and women who aimed to create a Western art aesthetic, and began exhibiting alongside them in American shows. She even got a write-up in the *New York Times* as a result, three lines that viciously dismissed her work. She was curiously proud of this. For one thing, the critic was of the old school and annoying him signalled to her that she was on the right track. Furthermore, any kind of critical success she had ever met with was inevitably followed by a shameful failure. Praise made her suspicious and uncomfortable. And the more she learned about the art world, the more she noticed that people found the idea of embattled, embittered artists rather noble. Emily fit perfectly into that slot, and her new group of friends seemed to admire her for it.

The good people of Victoria were still unconvinced, though they were beginning to be excited by all the national attention she was getting. One acquaintance told her she wanted to buy an Emily Carr canvas, not because she admired Emily's work, but as an investment before they turned into pricey collector's items. Emily's older sisters remained dour and disapproving. They flatout told her she was wasting her time.

Emily ignored them. Pottery-making and dog-breeding, her two most profitable business interests, were put aside to give her more time for painting and travelling. She resumed her northern excursions, though she found circumstances there had changed for the worse. The remaining totem poles were so rotted they were almost unpaintable, and the Native peoples were more likely to ignore her than welcome her the way they had in the past. She was no longer a novelty to them. Even her old friends Clara and William Russ claimed they were too busy to act as her guides. It was a disappointment, and Emily felt a little lost.

Lawren Harris thought he had the answer. They had begun exchanging letters as soon as she returned home, discussing art and religion. She liked to speak of the "intimacy" of their correspondence, though their relationship was in no way sexual. She felt she could speak candidly with him on any subject. He became a sort of guru to her, introducing her to nature-themed writers like Emerson and Whitman and encouraging her to study the highly esoteric Theosophist movement.

Emily had been fervently religious in the past. When she was a child, her father had conducted family prayers every morning before breakfast. She had been known to attend church twice on Sundays in her younger days, though she was scornful of her Bible-thumping sisters and had gradually cooled on organized religion as she grew older and more cynical.

She found Theosophy a little hard to follow, despite the books she gamely read on the subject. Harris presented it as the religion of artists, allowing them to find God not through the Bible, but through nature and their paintings. Emily thought at first there must be something to it, as her response to Harris's paintings had been a near-mystical experience. Her soul was touched by something "wonderful, mighty, not of this world" when she gazed on them. Perhaps he was on the right path. Her journals were full of her quest to get in touch with "the Infinite." But Emily slowly began to suspect that Theosophy was nonsense. She settled back into regular church attendance and the comfort of the religion she grew up with. She was so eager to please Harris, though, that she continued to feign interest long after she had given up on Theosophy. Her rejection of his religion was the beginning of a rift between them.

Harris did still have some good advice to give. He

told her that if the totem paintings continued to be so draining and frustrating, she should go back to nature and concentrate on her landscape paintings. Spirituality could be found everywhere in the natural world, not just in the Native totems.

She set out to paint the mountains, as her idol did, on day trips and longer excursions. In Pemberton, BC, she knocked herself out trekking miles along mountain trails, losing her way and panicking at the sight of fresh bear droppings. She lugged paints, paper, a stool, and a pack lunch while she wandered around in circles, lost. She was exhausted by the time she regained her bearings. She was now in her early 60s, overweight and out of shape. There had to be an easier way of getting around than this.

The Elephant
Emily's increasing profile had begun to benefit her in small ways. Her friend and supporter Edythe Hembroff had organized a drive to raise funds to buy a painting, *Kispiox Village* (also known as *Kispiox Totems*), which would then be donated to the provincial government. A tea party was held at the famed Empress Hotel to celebrate the acquisition. The formal affair thoroughly embarrassed Emily, but she also received a cheque for the princely sum of $166, for which she was supremely

grateful. It was enough to pay for two or three guided sketching trips, but those had become too exhausting. She needed to find another mode of transport

As a little girl, Emily had loved to make believe that she was one of a roaming band of Gypsies, travelling the land in a caravan. That may be why she noticed the decrepit old second-hand camper van on the side of the road, a For Sale sign hung in the window. It was not the most of elegant of vehicles — little better than a box on wheels — and it would have to be towed to wherever she wished to go, but with the *Kispiox Village* cheque burning a hole in her pocket, she could not resist realizing her childhood fantasy.

The Elephant or Mrs. Noah's Ark, as she liked to call it, was hardly a palace, though she fixed it up to be comfortable and homey. There was a bed, a writing table, a cooler, a little portable stove, and comfortable spots for her favourite creatures — Woo the monkey, Sophie the rat, and the latest batch of yapping dogs. Since she did not have a car and had to pay to have the thing towed, there was a limit to how far she could travel. Abandoned Native villages were out. Fields, parks, and campgrounds were in.

The Elephant gave her the luxury of time — her sketching trips could stretch into weeks instead of lasting for a few days — but it also meant an end to the

Emily with friends in her beloved caravan The Elephant, ca. 1934

solitude and silence she had enjoyed in her earlier rambles. In the old days, her only distraction might be a far-off porpoise splashing in the sea, or an eagle wheel-

ing through the sky. Now, other campers would swarm around at the novel sight of a monkey in a dress. They would pet the dogs, squeal over the rat. She felt like the freak show at a travelling circus. People would come up behind her as she settled down to sketch, something which always made her terribly uncomfortable, and ask a lot of nosy questions. In those Depression-era times, she was also occasionally bothered, even threatened, by itinerants seeking handouts of food or money.

The van was big enough for a human companion as well as herself and her pets, and sometimes a fellow artist like Edythe Hembroff would come along, or friends like Henry, a mentally handicapped boy she liked to mother. Her caravan camp-outs became minor social events as friends and family dropped by to picnic or relax for the day. Emily the misanthropist was hardly delighted, but Emily the extrovert secretly enjoyed the attention. It was often impossible to get any work done, but the visits subsided once the novelty of the van wore off.

Alone in the British Columbia forests that she loved, Emily became surprisingly lonely. She was producing good, strong, interesting work, but because she did not need to paint at the frantic pace she had maintained in the past, she had more time to absorb the atmosphere of the forest. The oppressive silence, the loneliness, even the beating of the rain on the roof of the caravan, all became slightly depressing to her. What was even worse was her growing estrangement from the men she used to revere, the Group of Seven.

Rebirth

Alone Again

Emily Carr was not a terribly happy woman. It is true that life had dealt her some hard blows, but she also had a cruel streak and an unpleasant tendency to sabotage her relationships with others. Her dealings with the Eastern artists had all the elements of an ill-fated love affair. In the beginning, her admiration of them bordered on drooling puppy love — she was certainly infatuated by Lawren Harris — and she was enormously proud to be associated with them when she was invited to contribute paintings to several of their shows.

Her demands on her Eastern counterparts could be excessive, however. Emily never had a manager or an agent. She relied instead on a network of friends and admirers to promote her work. Consequently, she had terrible trouble keeping track of who had sent what where, and this caused her a great deal of anxiety. If a painting did not sell, there could be a delay of two to three years before she got it back. She would become enraged and blame the person who had only been trying to help her in the first place. She began to sour on the idea of sending her works out East, thinking it was too much trouble and expense.

Emily was starting to feel disenchanted with the tight-knit Eastern art world as a whole. Lawren Harris, the group's unofficial leader, had nearly given up painting entirely by 1932 due to an increasingly complicated personal life. By the following year the Group of Seven had dissolved and renamed themselves the Canadian Group of Painters, losing much of their force and influence at the same time. Emily no longer felt included in their midst, and individual artists in the group began to be the focus of her wrath. A. Y. Jackson was a misogynist. Arthur Lismer was a "leaky old blowbag." She was certain they were making insulting comments about her behind her back.

It was pure paranoia for the most part, though Frederick Varley apparently really did hate her, calling her mannish and questioning her hygiene. Emily felt betrayed when she found out Lawren Harris was letting others read the highly personal letters she wrote to him. She was scandalized (and very likely jealous) when she found out he was divorcing his quiet, decent, non-threatening little wife and marrying Bess Housser, an artist in her own right and ex-wife of the man who had written *A Canadian Art Movement*, the book that had been Emily's introduction to the Group of Seven in the first place. Their correspondence continued for a while, and Emily would always be indebted to him, but something vital had been lost. She was on her own once again.

A New Direction

Emily was now well into her 60s, and it was starting to show. She was arthritic and beginning to lose her hearing in one ear. It was more difficult than ever to clamber up and down the stairs at the House of All Sorts, waiting hand and foot on her tenants. The caravan had served her well for four summers, but it too was becoming a burden, and she was tempted to get rid of both house and van. Her three oldest sisters were dead, disapproving of her until the end. Alice, her favourite, was still alive but slowly going blind.

The two sisters were closer now than they had ever been. After decades of ignoring her sister's work, Alice had finally relented and taken a good, hard look at Emily's sketches. She was stunned.

"They're beautiful," she marvelled. "No...they're wonderful," she said, and kissed her sister on the cheek.

Emily thought her heart would break with joy. The two now spent many happy hours drinking tea and reminiscing about old times.

She was an old lady, sick and on the wane, but the world had not seen the last of Emily Carr. She still had a lifetime of stories to tell...

Chapter 5
Final Days

The room was cold, white, antiseptic — except for the huge cluster of daffodils blooming in a vase, and the bold, sweeping sketches on a little table by the hospital bed. Emily had not felt this gloomy since her days back in the wards of the East Anglia Sanatorium. It was 1937 and this time it was her heart, not her head, that was the problem. She had been stuck at home the previous weekend, in terrible pain, but, stubborn as ever, had not wanted to call the doctor — "Not on a Sunday night!" Now her recovery was slow and sure. She was almost well enough to get up without someone chasing her around with a wheelchair and a hypodermic full of painkillers.

Her sister had promised to take care of her beloved creatures, but Alice's eyesight was fading and Emily was eager to get back to them. She was tired of the bland hospital food and wanted the warmth and comfort of her own kitchen. She could not wait to get home to her easel, where a half-finished canvas awaited her. She could not wait to get back to her writing desk, where her whole life was in the process of unfolding.

Leaving the House of All Sorts
Emily finally sold the House of All Sorts and bought a cottage on St. Andrews Street in Victoria. It was roughly the size of a postage stamp, nowhere near big enough to accommodate the decades of debris she had accumulated in the House of All Sorts. Her paintings had to be stored in specially constructed racks. The larger items that could not fit in her new home, old furniture and the like, had been auctioned off or given away. The smaller, more intimate possessions — photos, letters, old bills, and certificates from her dog-breeding years — were pulled out, looked at, sighed over, then packed away or thrown on the bonfire. Emily also burned old sketches and canvases, shameful things from the times when she had been confused about her purpose.

She felt little pangs of pleasure looking through some of those old letters, though. She had always felt so unloved, so alone, yet there had been stacks and stacks of correspondence, proof of how much she had mattered to so many people through all the years. It was a relief not to have any of her old love letters. She had consigned them to the flames long ago.

Woo was shrieking again, unhappy with the new arrangements. She was mostly confined to her cage these days and would soon be housed with others of her kind in the Vancouver Zoo. Emily would miss the dear little animal with her quirky personality and haunting eyes that were so like her own. She would have to find good homes for her entire menagerie. But now was not the time for sentimentality.

Emily morosely expected that the little house, so quiet and empty after the creaks and whispers and stomps and roars of the boarding house, would be the place she would die. Dying itself did not particularly worry her, but she hoped it would not be a long, drawn-out, shameful death, slowly losing her faculties in another hospital room. She had confided to a friend that she thought the elderly should not be patched up and sent home when they were terribly ill. Instead, she felt they should be allowed to die on their own, with dignity.

She did not think of herself as being in that dire a

state yet, though the doctors had issued an ominous warning. For the time being she was not allowed to paint. But unlike the ghastly English doctors, this time they had not forbidden Emily from indulging in all her passions. She was still allowed to write.

The Art of Words

Emily was carefully wrapped up in a shawl with a hot water bottle at her feet in order to keep any chills at bay. She expected to be well enough to get up any day now, though not yet. "These queer blobs beneath me are not my own feet yet," she sighed. Lying in bed with a few plumped-up pillows and her dog, Pout, cuddled beside her was wonderful, but she needed peace and quiet, even more so than when she was painting.

Emily had a notepad propped up on her lap and an old-fashioned fountain pen in her hand. She had two basic rules when writing: "Get to the point as directly as you can; never use a big word when a little one will do." She would drag herself over to the typewriter when she felt stronger and transcribe what she had written.

Several years ago she had convinced a friend to sign up for a summer school class with her. The course in short fiction was a huge step for her. As a child, she had kept a journal, but one of her sisters stole it, read it, and sneered at her because of it. When she found out

Lawren Harris was reading her letters to others, she had the same feeling of hurt and betrayal. She had not kept a consistent diary again until she was in her 60s. The thought of someone criticizing something she had written from the heart was painful for her. But she believed she had something to say, and the summer school class loosened her tongue. She had been writing non-stop since then.

As she lay huddled up in her sick bed, the stories she became most enthusiastic about were the vignettes describing her visits to the Native villages. She'd had to change some of the details — Clara and William Russ, her guides on her first trips north, became known as Louisa and Jimmie, just as her English friend Mrs. Redden became Mrs. Radcliffe in later tales. She carefully omitted the fact that her beloved friend Sophie Frank had ever been a prostitute. Some events had to be conflated, some dates had to be changed, and some stories were purely the product of her imagination. She made the changes partly for literary purposes, partly because she simply could not remember all the little details from so long ago, and partly to protect the innocent and the not-so-innocent. The need for authenticity that had informed her totem paintings and pottery-making was no longer a priority.

The stories that veered too far from her own experiences could be truly atrocious. "The Hully-up Paper," which tries to re-create the life of a Native family in crisis, has an unintentional patronizing tone that borders on the racially offensive. But Emily was none-the-less proud of her effort, so much so that she read an early version of it aloud at a gathering of other aspiring writers in 1934.

There was a sweetness behind the rest of the tales, though. It was such a joy for her to remember those days, wandering around with her paints in Ucluelet, Kispiox, or Alert Bay, especially now that she was mostly bedridden, and that joy shone through her words. She credited her storytelling with making her well again. Writing reminded her of why she had become an artist in the first place. She had associated Native peoples with nature, and nature with purity, exactly what she had wanted to represent in her paintings.

Her faulty memory was not the only flaw with her short stories, however. Emily never claimed to be an educated woman. She had come very close to being last in her class in elementary school and had dropped out of high school at 17. She never held a degree of any kind. Her spelling was atrocious, and if she could not come up with the right word, she would simply make one up. Her use of slang could make a person's eyes water. Her handwriting was terrible, and she would scribble notes, stories, and even letters to friends on pieces of scrap paper.

Always looking for the practical solution to her dilemmas, she had taken typing lessons at a local business school to aid her writing. The experience had been perfectly terrible. The old dog had considerable difficulty learning new tricks. Emily pecked away without ever improving, something that infuriated the woman who had accomplished so much in life simply by plugging away. She was a great deal older than the other students — young hussies of whom she disapproved and was slightly afraid. They seemed to have so much less fear than she ever did.

Emily frowned on the behaviour of modern girls. She had recently sat on the sidelines at a May Queen dance and was shocked by how much flesh young women were showing nowadays. The dresses they paraded around in were a scandal — "tighter and more suggestive than their own skins," she moaned. They were not like her Carol, who was a decent, moral girl.

Emily hated children. She had enjoyed teaching them when she was young, playful, and energetic, but when she grew old and cranky there was a mutual cooling in enthusiasm. Children loved Woo but were afraid of Emily, and she would scowl and swear to keep them from getting too close to her.

Final Days

Carol Williams had been one of the students boarding at the summer school where Alice Carr taught, and when Emily dropped by for a visit one day it was, she said, "love at first sight." It was a maternal love, but very twisted, and the relationship was alarming in its intensity. Emily became the girl's personal art instructor and shared her love of animals and nature with Carol. The two spent hours alone together, had special nicknames they would whisper in each other's ear, and shared a fantasy life that recalled Emily's magical memories of childhood. Carol began to call Emily "Mom" — which would have been fine if she had been an orphan, but her mother was very much alive. Emily even had the gall to approach Mrs. Williams and ask for permission to adopt the girl, so intense was the bond they shared. The other woman wisely said no, but Carol continued to send Emily cards and flowers on Mother's Day well into adulthood.

Carol and the long-suffering Edythe were not the only close friends in Emily's life. There was also Flora, a friend from summer school, who was Emily's "listening lady." For a long time it was Flora who would correct and revise Emily's stories for her. It was a huge job. Hoping for a little return on her devotion, Flora sent a stack of Emily's early stories to a variety of magazines. She never got a reply.

On the Radio

In 1936, Emily gained the services of a very helpful new friend. Ruth Humphreys was an English instructor at Victoria College. She agreed to review Emily's short stories — for a price. She demanded one of Emily's sketches in exchange.

As Ruth read through her new friend's work, she quickly lost interest in all the technical flaws. Those could be fixed. What really excited her was the content. There was a freshness about these stories that appealed to her.

She knew a man, formerly a professor at the University of British Columbia, who had quit his job and become the regional director for CBC Radio. He would know if the stories were as worthwhile as she suspected they were. And if magazine editors continued to refuse to accept the stories for publication, he might have a slightly more novel way of getting them out to the public.

Ira Dilworth was considerably younger than Emily, but they had a lot in common — similar tastes, similar background. Emily vaguely remembered Ira as a young man, pushing a lawn mower around a neighbour's front yard, and she had slightly less fond memories of an encounter with him at an exhibition of hers in the late 1920s, when he had been one of the disbelievers who had mocked her work in her presence.

Now that they were re-acquainted, they quickly established a solid working relationship. Dilworth became Emily's "honorary editor," guiding her line by line through her stories, correcting her errors, but never letting her feel that he was interfering with her storytelling. Mutual trust and respect quickly developed, only to give way to something more.

Writer and editor wrote to one another constantly. Most of their early letters were concerned with Emily's literary efforts. Then the tone began to change. They became more emotional and even passionate. Emily was coy in her letters to Ira, referring to herself in the third person and talking baby talk to him. She pestered him for approval and feedback on dozens of her stories. While he held down a full-time job and engaged in literary pursuits of his own, he was so devoted to Emily that he was only too happy to oblige. Like Emily, Dilworth was unmarried, though he had adopted his niece Phylis, of whom Emily became very jealous.

Emily called him "Eye" and signed her letters using the special nickname he had given her, "Small." They vowed their deepest love for one another. They even exchanged rings, though not in any remotely formal ceremony. If Emily's relationship with Carol Williams was intense, her friendship with Ira Dilworth bordered on insane; it made her hero-worship of Lawren Harris look like a high school crush. Despite all appearances to the contrary, however, their May-December romance was a purely platonic friendship.

Small had plenty of reasons to love Eye. He acted as her unpaid editor and agent. He was also her greatest fan. With his influence at the CBC, he decided that putting her stories on the air would be a clever way to introduce her work as a writer to the public. Emily was delighted; she was a radio fanatic. Her favourites were the soap operas that ran every week, clean and wholesome programs that have little in common with the steamy serials of today. She drove everyone crazy as she blasted the volume to compensate for her increasing deafness.

Her charming stories of childhood and Native life were the perfect fare for Canadian audiences. Like her favourite soaps, they provided relief to a nation that had recently entered World War II.

In 1940, the first of Emily's short stories were read on air. Not by Emily herself, mind you. She liked a little attention, not a lot. Public speaking was not her favourite thing. She had given a few lectures in her life, and they had always been dismal affairs. Her misery was obvious to all as she read her notes flatly, without looking up at the audience. In a blatantly Freudian mix-up, she had once dropped her folded-up lecture notes into a collection plate at church, only to keep the envelope with her offering in it in her pocket. Keeping her away from the CBC studios was the smartest way for Ira Dilworth to sell her image to the public.

A Canadian Success Story

For possibly the first time in her life, Emily had a smashing success without any hideous consequences. Everyone loved her stories. Ordinary people came up to her on the street to tell her how much they had enjoyed listening to them. They were reminded of when they were children; they were reminded they were Canadian.

Emily was genuinely happy. It was exactly what she wanted. Positive reviews in the press meant less than nothing to her; the praise of her peers she greeted with suspicion. Critics and intellectuals always had agendas, and Emily was tired of playing games. She was thrilled to connect with the people in the street. When she went to buy groceries and the clerk told her he enjoyed her stories, she could be certain he meant it.

It reminded her of an experiment she once conducted. In the mid-1930s, one of her grand plans was to take art appreciation out of the hands of the experts and create a "People's Gallery," an unpretentious place where ordinary folks of any class and culture could drop by and enjoy the paintings. It was partly an education

endeavour and partly to thumb her nose at her old ene-
mies, the Arts and Crafts Society, whose membership
was selective. She had managed to drum up a fair
amount of support for her gallery from a variety of quar-
ters, but funding was a problem: there wasn't any. She
gamely opened her own studio to the public to show
how easily her idea could be realized, but it did not draw
huge crowds. It quickly fizzled out. What she had not
been able to do then with her art, she had now done
with her writing.

The radio stories were not just popular with the
public. Publishers began to come around. In 1941, the
year she turned 70, Emily's first collection of short
stories was published. The title was *Klee Wyck*, her
nickname from the Ucluelet days. She dedicated it to
her friend Sophie Frank. The book was a bestseller and
a critical success. It won the prestigious Governor
General's award for non-fiction in 1941. Suddenly Emily
Carr's name was on everyone's lips, and not merely as an
intriguing oddity.

The people of Victoria, who had scorned her for so
long, finally embraced her. An organization called the
Women's Canadian Club held a joint book launch and
70th birthday party for her in Victoria. She was shocked
when she arrived and the place was packed. The SPCA,
knowing of her reputation as an animal lover, had sent a

representative. The premier sent an official letter acknowledging her contribution to the arts in British Columbia. Even members of the Arts and Crafts Society, her old nemesis, showed up to honour her. She got a huge cake and a kiss on the cheek from Ira Dilworth. Emily was stunned by the outpouring of affection. It was a huge turnaround from the times when she felt the entire city was ignoring and patronizing her.

Klee Wyck would remain her most popular book, but she was encouraged to keep writing and published two more works in quick succession. *The Book of Small* was another bestseller, this time containing short, dreamy pieces focussing on her childhood. It was the choice of many publications for book of the year in 1942, though Alice Carr was upset over what she felt was an unflattering family portrait. Emily, still bitter despite all her success, had her revenge on all the tenants who had ever annoyed her when she released her reminiscences in *The House of All Sorts* two years later.

The books were not just well received, they were loved. It was an extraordinary comeback. People began throwing the word "genius" around. Emily was no longer a quaint regional painter of Native life, she was a national celebrity.

Emily Carr

Triumphant Final Days

Respect and public acclaim were all very well, but Emily had not given up being a painter. The last few years of her life were extraordinarily productive, especially considering her worsening health. In her youth she had wanted to paint for selfish reasons, but now she wanted to keep working for noble motives: for Canada and for other female artists. By the 1940s she was having major solo exhibitions at home and abroad and doing something she had never done before: earning a living from her artwork alone. Even being a successful author was never enough to make her rich.

In true Emily style, she was more bewildered by this turn of events than gratified. In her journal she totted up the amount she made from the sale of five canvases — over $1000 — with the simple comment "Goodness!" written at the end. Her gratitude increased once her ill health meant frequent hospital stays. Finally, she could pay her bills without making any huge personal sacrifices. She recognized that success was a gift. She was comfortable enough that she could start giving away her paintings to her friends, in recognition of their loyalty to her throughout the lean years.

She was still painting well after it would have been wise to stop. She continued her treks into the forest right up until 1942, when she was on the brink of requiring chronic care. She begged Ira Dilworth and Lawren Harris to tell her if the quality of her work began to deteriorate but, amazingly, it had not slipped at all. Harris even seemed a little giddy about the new works she was producing.

Some critics believe that in her final years she was at the height of her powers, that the lonesome windswept forest scenes are her very best work, rather than the more popular brooding totem paintings. Her light, swirling brushwork looked familiar to some. She was favourably compared more than once to Van Gogh. "Poor Van Gogh!" was her rueful response, though she was clearly very pleased. He was one of the few painters that Emily revered.

In another twist of fate, Emily began to be recognized in the land where she'd had her first, most shameful failure. The National Gallery organized an exhibition entitled "A Century of Canadian Art" and took it to London's prestigious Tate gallery. Both the London *Times* and the *Manchester Guardian* took note of Emily's contributions and gave her work rave reviews. Her old friend Eric Brown from the National Gallery made sure she was aware of this long-overdue recognition. Emily pretended not to care, though deep down she must have felt vindicated.

BC Archives E-01422

Emily's studio in her home in St. Andrews Street, ca. 1945

Final Days

Illness and Loss

Emily Carr's life did not end with the speed and dignity she had hoped for.

Her final years were marked by a series of triumphs and misfortunes. Her success as a writer did not make her complacent, and her health problems did not make her lazy. She could have been forgiven for taking to her bed and living out the rest of her life as an invalid, but after she recovered from her first batch of heart problems she continued to paint and write.

She had a frightening second stroke, which did not kill her, but did make real one of her greatest fears. She was incapacitated — paralyzed and unable to speak. It was terrifying, but short-lived. She was out of hospital in months, her recovery almost complete. Her face was numb on one side and she had trouble walking, but her mind was intact. Hating the thought of using a wheelchair, she had casters attached to a wooden butter crate and would perch on top of it and roll her way around the house. It was one way of continuing to assert control over her life. She was still feisty — she threatened to give Hitler a black eye if she ever met him — and she continued to work as hard as she could.

Her next episode was more severe. This time she lay in her hospital bed, babbling incoherently. Visitors could just about make out Woo's name. Her recovery came more slowly this time. She was not just in pain, she was frightened. She was encouraged to paint from her hospital bed as part of her therapy, but could barely lift up her brush. Her mind remained cloudy. She wrote letters to Ira Dilworth that made very little sense.

She recovered from this attack as well, but the woman who prized her independence would now require constant medical supervision. She had to enter a nursing home and use a despised wheelchair. It was the beginning of her final decline.

Fluid began to gather in Emily's chest as she lay helpless in the nursing home bed. She must have thought of her dying mother as she listed to her own shallow gasping breaths. She had time enough to arrange her affairs and receive one last visit from the people she cared about most: Lawren Harris, Ira Dilworth, and her last living sister, Alice.

Emily summoned up the strength to paint one final picture. It was a portrait of Woo. There was no pretty dress, her chain was gone, and she was not trapped behind the iron bars of a zoo cage. She was peering, with familiar cat-like eyes, from the gnarled shadows of a dark, imposing forest.

Epilogue
Emily Carr, Mythmaker

Emily Carr liked to pretend that she thought her fame was a fleeting thing, but in truth she believed otherwise. Before she died in 1945, she began to make the arrangements that would ensure that her life and work would never be forgotten.

Emily was sure that she had chosen the right men to help her in her quest. First, there was the Emily Carr Trust, of which Lawren Harris was trustee. Her entire artistic output would be left in their care. Harris, perhaps trying to protect her reputation, went through her sketches and paintings and threw out a huge number of early works. Fortunately, most were salvaged, and a key part of her legacy was preserved. Most of the works were then sold or disposed of in other ways. Of the rest, 45 of the best would be put aside and donated to the Vancouver Art Gallery, on permanent loan.

Ira Dilworth would be her literary editor. He was

bequeathed boxes of scribbled notepads, badly typed notes, and half-completed stories. He came through admirably. Emily had had three books published in her lifetime; three more were released posthumously.

Together, the two men would construct a splendid monument to her talent. But it was Alice, her sister, and Carol Williams, her surrogate daughter, who made the most moving gestures in Emily Carr's honour. Carol wrote of how she took a box of personal mementoes of Emily's, including an unidentified man's cufflinks, and buried them in an anonymous pot in Beacon Hill Park, a favourite haunt of Emily's since childhood. The box has never been found. Alice, meanwhile, had something a little more permanent in mind. She used some of the money Emily had left to her and had a bridge in the same park dedicated to her sister's memory.

* * *

Emily Carr never earned much of a living from her painting. For most of her lifetime she was ignored and insulted. But times have changed. Her paintings no longer appear bizarre and offensive, but are seen as a wonderful exploration of the Canadian West. Today, her canvases can fetch over a million dollars at auction, and her reputation continues to grow. At last, Emily Carr has emerged as a true Canadian icon.

Bibliography

Blanchard, Paula. *The Life of Emily Carr.* Vancouver/ Toronto: Douglas & McIntyre, 1987.

Carr, Emily. *The Complete Writings of Emily Carr.* Revised ed. Vancouver/Toronto: Douglas & McIntyre, 1997.

Hembrof-Schleicher, Edythe. *M.E.: A Portrayal of Emily Carr.* Toronto/Vancouver: Clarke, Irwin Co., Ltd., 1969

Shadbolt, Doris. *The Art of Emily Carr.* Vancouver/ Toronto: Douglas & McIntyre, 1979.

———. *Emily Carr.* Vancouver/Toronto: Douglas & McIntyre, 1990.

Tippett, Maria. *Emily Carr, a biography.* Toronto: Stoddart Publishing, 1979.

Acknowledgments

The author acknowledges the excellent work of Maria Tippett in *Emily Carr, a biography* for the quotes contained in this book. Thanks are due to Kathryn Bridge of the British Columbia Archives for her insightful comments on a draft of the manuscript.

All photographs are reproduced with permission from the British Columbia Archives.

About the Author

Cat Klerks has a degree in English from McGill University and a lifelong fascination with Canadian art. She lives and works in Banff, Alberta.

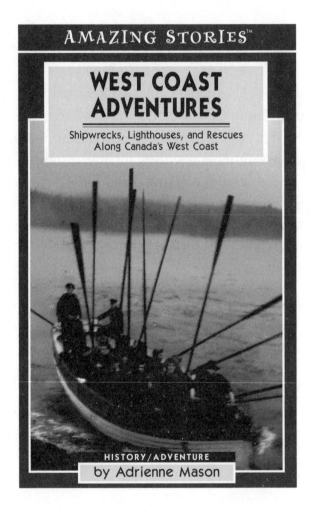

AMAZING STORIES™

VANCOUVER'S OLD-TIME SCOUNDRELS

Gassy Jack's Exploits and Other Skulduggery

HISTORY/BIOGRAPHY

by Jill Foran

Vancouver's Old-time Scoundrels
ISBN 1-55153-989-6

AMAZING STORIES™

MARY SCHÄFFER

An adventurous woman's
exploits in the Canadian Rockies

HISTORY/BIOGRAPHY
by Jill Foran

Mary Schäffer
ISBN 1-55153-999-3

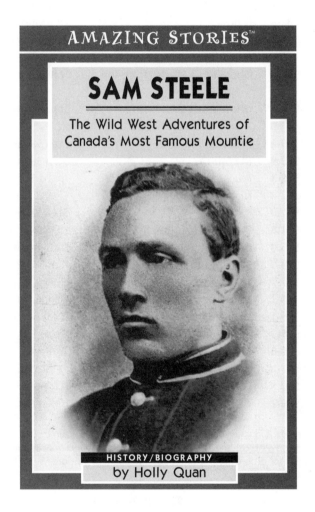

AMAZING STORIES™

SAM STEELE

The Wild West Adventures of
Canada's Most Famous Mountie

HISTORY/BIOGRAPHY
by Holly Quan

Sam Steele
ISBN 1-55153-997-7

OTHER AMAZING STORIES

ISBN	Title	Author
1-55153-977-2	Air Force War Heroes	Cynthia Faryon
1-55153-983-7	Alberta Titans	Susan Warrender
1-55153-982-9	Dinosaur Hunters	Lisa Murphy-Lamb
1-55153-970-5	Early Voyageurs	Marie Savage
1-55153-968-3	Edwin Alonzo Boyd	Nate Hendley
1-55153-992-6	Ghost Town Stories from the Red Coat Trail	Johnnie Bachusky
1-55153-993-4	Ghost Town Stories from the Canadian Rockies	Johnnie Bachusky
1-55153-969-1	Klondike Joe Boyle	Stan Sauerwein
1-55153-979-9	Ma Murray	Stan Sauerwein
1-55153-999-3	Mary Schäffer	Jill Foran
1-55153-962-4	Niagara Daredevils	Cheryl MacDonald
1-55153-981-0	Rattenbury	Stan Sauerwein
1-55153-991-8	Rebel Women	Linda Kupecek
1-55153-995-0	Rescue Dogs	Dale Portman
1-55153-998-5	Romance in the Rockies	Kim Mayberry
1-55153-997-7	Sam Steele	Holly Quan
1-55153-985-3	Tales from the Backcountry	Dale Portman
1-55153-986-1	Tales from the West Coast	Adrienne Mason
1-55153-994-2	The Heart of a Horse	Gayle Bunney
1-55153-989-6	Vancouver's Old-Time Scoundrels	Jill Foran
1-55153-987-X	Wilderness Tales	Peter Christensen
1-55153-990-X	West Coast Adventures	Adrienne Mason
1-55153-980-2	Women Explorers	Helen Rolfe

These titles are available wherever you buy books. If you have trouble finding the book you want, call the Altitude order desk at 1-800-957-6888, e-mail your request to: orderdesk@altitudepublishing.com or visit our Web site at www.amazingstories.ca

All titles retail for $9.95 Cdn or $7.95 US. (Prices subject to change.)

New AMAZING STORIES titles are published every month. If you would like more information, e-mail your name and mailing address to: amazingstories@altitudepublishing.com.